KU-275-221

KINGFISHER EXPLORER BOOKS

THE WORLD OF SPEED

Jonathan Rutland

Designed by David Nash

Illustrators
**Mike Atkinson · Ron Jobson · Brian Knight · Cliff Meadway
Doug Post · Ross Wardle · Craig Warwick · Mike Tregenza**

KINGFISHER BOOKS

In the 1900s machines have made high-speed travel part of our daily lives. Many people are fascinated by speed. And since ancient times racing has been one of the most popular sports. Today, people all over the world enjoy speed sports, especially motor racing. This takes various forms, including grand prix racing, speedway and motocross. But the thrills and the danger remain the same. Together, man and machine race to be first, to be the fastest.

Before the steam engine was invented, the horse-drawn chariot was the fastest vehicle. It could keep up a speed of about 35 km/h.

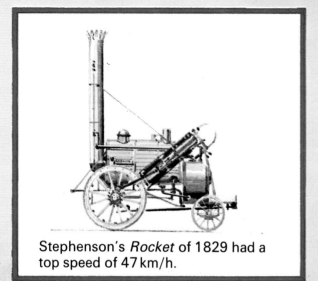
Stephenson's *Rocket* of 1829 had a top speed of 47 km/h.

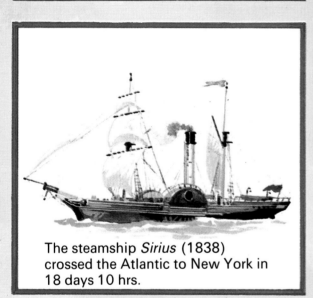
The steamship *Sirius* (1838) crossed the Atlantic to New York in 18 days 10 hrs.

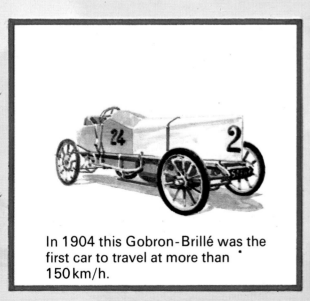
In 1904 this Gobron-Brillé was the first car to travel at more than 150 km/h.

Man on the Move

Less than two hundred years ago the fastest way to travel was on horseback, just as it had been in ancient times. Then the steam locomotive was invented and the railway age began.

The first public steam railway was the Stockton and Darlington railway in England. When it was opened in 1825, George Stephenson's *Locomotion* hauled a load of 91 tonnes at a speed of 11 km/h. Within 20 years trains could travel at more than 100 km/h and rail travel had become very popular. During the 1800s the steam locomotive was the 'king of speed' throughout the world.

The steam engine was used to power ships as early as 1783 when the *Pyroscaphe* built by the Marquis Claude de Jouffroy steamed up the river Saône in France. But it was many years before steamships could beat sailing vessels with a following wind.

Steam engines were also fitted to 'horseless carriages' on the road. But early cars were slow and clumsy. It was the invention of the petrol-driven car in 1885 that led to high-speed travel by road. It also led to a much faster method of travel. The petrol engine was light enough to make powered flight possible.

5

Speed on Rails

Modern electric and diesel trains can travel over 200 km/h. The world's fastest passenger train is the French National Railway's TGV *(Train à Grande Vitesse)* which means 'high-speed train'. It is made of lightweight materials and has powerful electric motors. The TGV can hurtle along at up to 270 km/h. It has automatic brakes to make it easier and safer to drive.

Another French train, the TGV-PSE has run even faster. It reached 380 km/h on a test run. Trains have even been tried with jet engines. The French Aérotrain runs on a single track. It rides on a cushion of air and its top speed is 387 km/h. But its engines are very noisy.

Rocket trains are faster still. But they are not suitable for carrying passengers. An exciting new idea is to use magnetic drive. The train is moved long by magnets, and is held just *above* the track. The magnetic train makes no noise and has reached over 500 km/h on a test run with passengers.

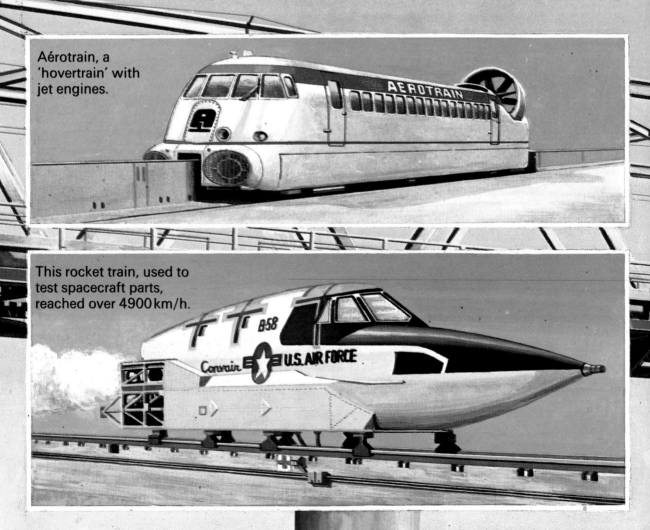

Aérotrain, a 'hovertrain' with jet engines.

This rocket train, used to test spacecraft parts, reached over 4900 km/h.

This French train is the world record holder on ordinary track. It reached 330.9 km/h in 1955.

The Tokaido express or 'bullet' train is the world's first very fast passenger service. It runs between Okayama and Osaka in Japan, travelling at up to 250 km/h.

7

Meadway

The Martini Porsche 936 –
winner of Le Mans 24
hours race 1977 with an
average speed of
193.6 km/h.

Speed on the Road

In the early days of motoring
some of the fastest cars had electric or steam engines. For a short
time a steam car called *Wogglebug*
was the world's fastest vehicle. In
1907 it reached a speed of 241
km/h.

Today almost all cars have
petrol engines. The fastest racing
cars are quite small but have huge
wheels. Their bodies are low and
smooth so that air passes round
them easily, without slowing them
down. To stop them skidding,
the cars have small upside-down
wings called aerofoils. As the air
rushes over them, it pushes the
car down and keeps the wheels on
the road.

Cars built specially to break
speed records are driven by jet
and rocket engines. The world
land speed record of more than
1019 km/h is held by *Thrust 2*, a
jet-engined car driven by Richard
Noble on the Black Rock Desert
in Nevada, USA in 1983.

BEVELOR

MARTINI

The Blue Flame, a rocket-powered car driven by Gary Gabelich, set its world record of 1016 km/h on the Bonneville Salt Flats in Utah, USA in 1970.

FLAME

The large picture on this page shows a Grand Prix motor race. The drivers need all their skill to keep their cars on the track as they race round corners.

The fastest racing car, the Porsche 917/30, can reach a speed of around 400 km/h.

A hydrofoil has V-shaped underwater 'wings'. Only the tips of the wings ride through the water. The fastest hydrofoils have three wings and an electric 'eye' to measure the height of the waves ahead. A computer sets the wings so that the hydrofoil rides smoothly over the water. Most hydrofoils are used on large rivers.

In 1955, Donald Campbell set up a new water speed record of more than 300 km/h in his jet-powered speedboat *Bluebird*. In 1967, *Bluebird* streaked across a lake at 527 km/h before it overturned. Donald Campbell was killed.

Speed in Water

A ship travelling on the water cannot go faster than about 90 km/h. But a craft which skims along (or above) the surface can travel at much higher speeds. Craft which can do this are hydrofoils, hovercraft and hydroplanes.

A hydrofoil rests in the water at low speed. But as it goes faster it is lifted up until it skims along on legs rather like skis. This cuts down the 'drag' of the water. Hydrofoils can travel at around 110 km/h.

Hovercraft travel on a cushion of air. Powerful fans push air downwards, and lift the craft above the waves. A big passenger-carrying hovercraft speeds along at up to 142 km/h.

Even faster is the racing hydroplane. This speedboat can skim or 'plane' across calm water so fast it almost flies.

a large passenger-carrying hovercraft

Concorde, the Anglo-French supersonic jet airliner, can travel at over 2000 km/h. It crosses the Atlantic in under 3 hours.

The Lockheed SR-71A, the fastest jet aircraft.

6063

Meadway

RACING CARS

Some early racing cars have become classics because of their many successes. The Locomobile Old 16 was the first American car to challenge and beat European racers. It could travel at up to 177 km/h. The Bugatti Type 35 was the most successful Grand Prix racer ever. This car could reach 201 km/h. One of the top Italian racers, the Alfa Romeo Type 158 won nearly all of the races it entered. Its top speed was 307.7 km/h. The Auto-Union, a German car, won most of the 1936 Grand Prix races.

Other racing cars are famous for their special features. The Chaparral 2F was the first 'winged' racing car. Most racing cars have wings or aerofoils on the front and back.

The best racing cars today are Formula 1 Grand Prix cars. Although they have many similar features, the shape of the bodywork varies slightly from car to car. Grand Prix races are often won on reliability rather than speed because there is so much strain on the mechanical parts of the cars when they are constantly run at high speeds. The Brabham BT53, the Alfa Romeo 185T, the McLaren MP4/2B and the Williams FW10 Honda are Formula 1 Grand Prix cars.

To remove the panorama wall poster carefully lift the ends of each staple with a small pair of scissors. Take the poster from the book and then press the ends of the staples back into place.

CARS

LOCOMOBILE OLD 16
1906

WILLIAMS FW10 HONDA
1985

ALFA ROMEO 185T
1985

BRABHAM BT53
1984

AUTO-UNION
1936

The fastest aeroplane ever was the rocket-powered North American X-15A which reached 7297 km/h.

Speed in the Air

The first aeroplanes were slow and clumsy. They had small petrol engines driving propellers, and their top speed was about 30 km/h. Later planes could fly much faster. But propeller-driven planes never reached speeds of more than about 800 km/h.

It was the invention of the jet engine that made higher speeds possible. But the first plane to fly faster than the speed of sound (about 1100 km/h) was the rocket-powered Bell X-1 in 1947.

A modern jet warplane, like the Lockheed SR-71A, can fly at more than 3500 km/h. At this speed the pilot has little time to think. Computers and other electronic instruments help him fly the plane safely.

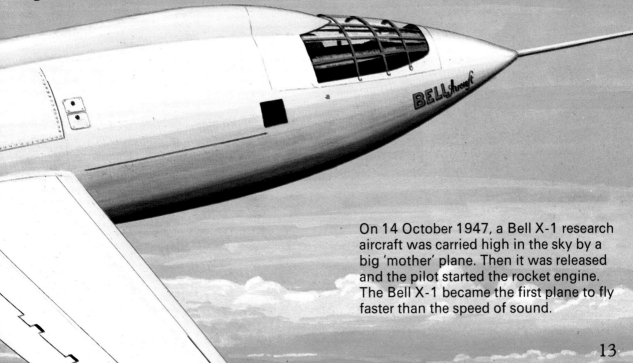

On 14 October 1947, a Bell X-1 research aircraft was carried high in the sky by a big 'mother' plane. Then it was released and the pilot started the rocket engine. The Bell X-1 became the first plane to fly faster than the speed of sound.

Frontiers of Speed

The fastest human travellers ever were three American astronauts. They were in an Apollo spacecraft returning from the Moon. There is no air in space to slow down a spacecraft. And the Earth's gravity pulls a returning space-craft towards it, faster and faster. The astronauts reached the amazing speed of 39,897 km/h.

The fastest recorded speed of a spacecraft is 240,000 km/h, set by a US-German probe called Helios B, travelling towards the sun. But Pioneer 10, a robot probe, is the first spacecraft to travel fast enough to break out of the solar system. It flew past Jupiter in 1973 at 173,214 km/h, and in 1983 sped beyond Pluto.

Even at these speeds, a journey to the distant planets takes years. And far beyond the planets lie the stars. Most stars are so far away that the light from them takes many years to reach us.

Yet light is the fastest thing we know about. It travels 299,792 km in just one second. Light from the Sun takes 8 minutes to reach Earth. We cannot make a space-craft travel at this amazing speed. Scientists think nothing can travel faster than the speed of light.

Pioneer spacecraft

An Apollo spacecraft on its way to the Moon. To escape the Earth's gravity the rocket must reach a speed of 39,580 km/h. On the return journey, the spacecraft has to reach a speed of only 8500 km/h to escape from the weaker 'pull' of the Moon.

People at Speed

Alone, man cannot move faster than his legs will carry him. The best sprinters in the world cannot run faster than about 40 km/h and the best swimmers cannot move through the water at more than a brisk walking pace. But muscle power can be used to reach much higher speeds in other sports. Among the fastest are ice-skating, cycling and skiing. With the help of gravity -- the downward pull of the Earth – skiers can speed down steep snow-covered slopes at more than 100 km/h. But the fastest speeds of all are reached in the daring sport of sky-diving.

The sky-diver jumps from a plane high above the ground. The pull of the Earth's gravity makes him fall. But as he falls faster and faster the air pushes up more and more against him until the 'pull' is balanced by the 'push'. So the diver falls steadily at about 300 km/h until he opens his parachute. At great heights where the air is thin, divers have reached 1000 km/h.

SPEED SPORTS

RUNNING The fastest sprinter in the world reached 44.88 km/h over a few metres. But the record over 100 metres is only 36.16 km/h.

SKATING Ice hockey players skate at up to 47 km/h and the puck (the 'ball') is hit at speeds of up to 190 km/h.

CYCLING This is the fastest 'man-powered' sport. The cycling speed record is just over 81 km/h.

SKIING Racing skiers often reach over 100 km/h and the record speed is almost 209 km/h.

sky-diving

Speed in Nature

Animals need speed for two reasons – to catch food or to escape being caught. The fastest creatures on land, in the sea, and in the air are all hunters.

The fastest of all is a bird, the spine-tailed swift. It flies at up to 170 km/h chasing insects. Spine-tailed swifts spend most of their time in the air. They live on rock ledges and 'take off' by diving into the air.

Golden eagles and peregrine falcons can reach speeds of over 100 km/h when diving after their prey. And at sea frigate birds may be

The spine-tailed swift is the fastest creature in the world.

cheetah

blown along in a gale at even higher speeds.

The fastest fish is the sailfish. Its slim body can slice through the water at more than 100 km/h. At speed, the sailfish folds its sail-like fin down into a groove in its back. This makes it even more stream-lined.

The cheetah is the fastest mammal. It can reach about 135 km/h in a short sprint. But some antelopes and gazelles are better long-distance runners. The pronghorn antelope can keep going at a steady 56 km/h for many minutes.

The sailfish is the fastest creature in the sea.

pronghorn
antelope

Faster than the Eye

When a horse gallops, its legs move too quickly for our eyes to see each one clearly. All we see is a blur. No one knew for sure how a galloping horse's legs moved until the camera was invented in the 1800s. Then a photographer called Eadweard Muybridge took a lot of photographs of a galloping horse. His camera 'froze' each moment, and he could see how the horse's legs moved.

When we watch a film, we see pictures of people and things moving on the screen. But the film is made up of 'still' pictures. Each photo or 'frame' shows one moment frozen by the camera. The frames follow one another so quickly that our eyes cannot pick out each one. By running the film at the right speed, the pictures seem to move.

'High-speed' photography shows us many things which happen faster than our eyes can see. Without it, judges could not tell the winners of close horse races. In a 'photo-finish', the horses are photographed as they speed past the winning post.

A high-speed camera can freeze the rapid wing-beat of a hovering humming-bird. It can also show us a bullet leaving a gun, and how a golf ball is squashed as the club hits it. The fastest cameras can take many thousands of pictures a second. But nothing in the world is as fast as the light we need to see anything at all.

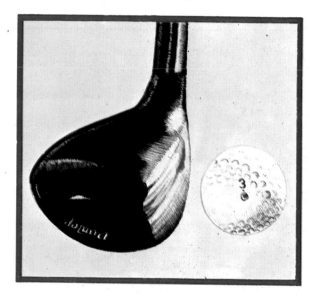

The pictures show some of the things that happen too fast for the eye to see but which can be captured by the camera.

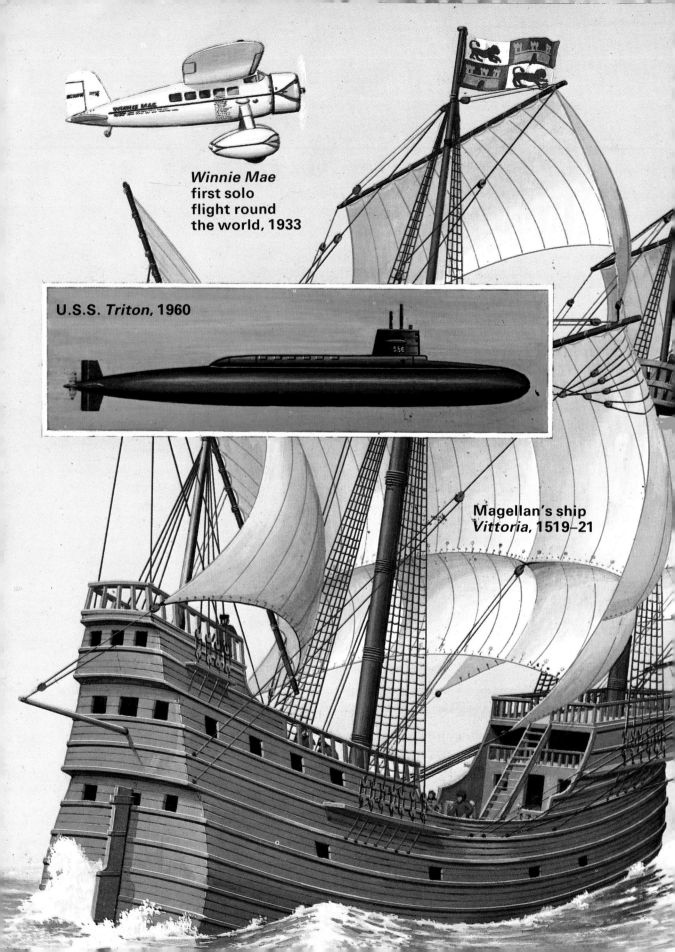

Winnie Mae
first solo
flight round
the world, 1933

U.S.S. *Triton*, 1960

Magellan's ship
Vittoria, 1519–21

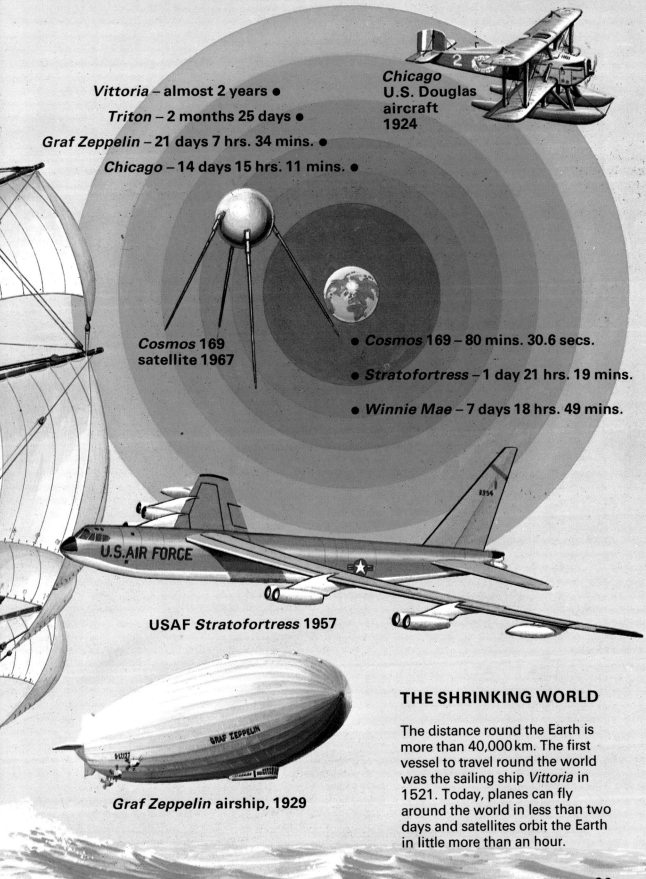

Vittoria – almost 2 years ●

Triton – 2 months 25 days ●

Graf Zeppelin – 21 days 7 hrs. 34 mins. ●

Chicago – 14 days 15 hrs. 11 mins. ●

Chicago
U.S. Douglas
aircraft
1924

Cosmos 169
satellite 1967

● *Cosmos* 169 – 80 mins. 30.6 secs.

● *Stratofortress* – 1 day 21 hrs. 19 mins.

● *Winnie Mae* – 7 days 18 hrs. 49 mins.

USAF *Stratofortress* 1957

Graf Zeppelin airship, 1929

THE SHRINKING WORLD

The distance round the Earth is more than 40,000 km. The first vessel to travel round the world was the sailing ship *Vittoria* in 1521. Today, planes can fly around the world in less than two days and satellites orbit the Earth in little more than an hour.

Index

Numbers in *italics* refer to illustrations.

This revised expanded edition published in 1987 by Kingfisher Books Limited, Elsley Court, 20–22 Great Titchfield Street, London W1P 7AD A Grisewood & Dempsey Company Originally published in small format paperback by Pan Books Ltd in 1978.

© Grisewood & Dempsey Ltd 1978, 1987

All rights reserved. No part of this publication may be reproduced, stored in a retrieval system or transmitted by any means, electronic, mechanical, photocopying or otherwise, without the prior permission of the publisher.

Cover designed by The Pinpoint Design Company

BRITISH LIBRARY CATALOGUING IN PUBLICATION DATA
Rutland, Jonathan
    The world of speed. – rev. ed –
    (Kingfisher explorer books)
    1. Speed – Juvenile literature
    I. Title   II. Rutland, Jonathan. Exploring the world of speed
    531'.112   QC127.4

    ISBN 0-86272-306-X

Phototypeset by Southern Positives and Negatives (SPAN), Lingfield, Surrey
Printed by Graficas Reunidas SA, Madrid, Spain